Scottish Paganism

AND

LGBTQIA+ Sexuality

THOMAS LANTING

GREEN MAGIC

Scottish Paganism © 2024 by Thomas Lanting.
All rights reserved. No part of this book may be used
or reproduced in any form without written
permission of the Author, except in the case
of quotations in articles and reviews.

GREEN MAGIC
Seed Factory
Aller
Langport
Somerset
TA10 0QN
England
www.greenmagicpublishing.com

Designed and typeset by Carrigboy, Wells, UK.
www.carrigboy.co.uk

ISBN 978 1 915580 17 7

GREEN MAGIC

THOMAS LANTING

LGBTQIA+ Officer
Scottish Pagan Federation

Dedicated to:

My parents, Egbert & Patricia Lanting.
Thank you always for your love.

My amazing husband, Iain Robertson.
My brothers, Ciaron & Sean.

Lastly to Mandy, Chris, Cherrie & Tiffany.
In memory of my godparents, Ken & Robyn.

Contents

PROLOGUE – Previous Presiding Officer –
John Macintyre 9

FOREWORD – Paganism & Sexuality –
My Journey – *Thomas Lanting* 13

1. The SPF – Sexuality & Diversity 17
2. The Roots of Sexual Diversity in Ancient World Beliefs 23
3. Sexuality in Magic 29
4. Advances in Sexual Inclusiveness Throughout the SPF's History 33
5. Marriage Equality & Interfaith Networking 37
6. Twenty Years of Scottish Government and its Impact on Sexuality 41
7. Sexuality & Discrimination 45
8. Sexuality & Mental Heath – Mental Health & Well-being Officer – *Matt Cormack* 53

CONTENTS

9. An A-Z Understanding of Sexuality – Scientific & Medical Descriptions ... 65

10. An Understanding of Sexuality Through the Eyes of the LGBTQIA+ Community ... 69

11. Nouns & Pronouns – Why are they Important? ... 79

12. Why we Need Allies & How to be One ... 83

13. LGBTQIA+ Deities ... 87

EPILOGUE – Current Presiding Officer – *Stephen Haggerty* ... 95

APPENDIX – References, Resources & Bibliography ... 103

Prologue

John Macintyre
Previous Presiding Officer

The Scottish Pagan Federation (SPF), like the original PF (Pagan Federation) it developed from, was initially focussed almost exclusively on campaigning for religious equality for Pagans and on countering defamation of Paganism. However, that in itself led naturally into embracing the wider Equalities agenda. This should not surprise us. Paganism has always celebrated diversity in both human beings and in Nature generally as good in itself, and the Equalities agenda has always been rooted in respect for diversity. Paganism is not homophobic. It does not encourage prejudice against gay, lesbian, bisexual or transgendered people, and values all adult, consensual and loving relationships equally. Paganism and Equalities have always made a good fit. Consequently, from the very beginning, the Scottish Pagan Federation did not discriminate on grounds of sexual orientation or gender and welcomed same-sex couples, and also polyamorous group relationships, as Joint Members on the same basis as everyone else.

Scottish PF's commitment to Equalities became much stronger with the election of Louise Park, first as Deputy Presiding Officer and later as Presiding Officer. Louise's earlier experience in negotiating legal recognition of Pagan Religious Marriage under Scots Law gave her the skills and connections to be a highly effective campaigner for Equal marriage rights for same-sex couples. Scottish PF quickly became a highly effective partner in the Faith in Marriage coalition of progressive faith & belief groups, and Equal Marriage passed into Scots Law in the spring of 2014. This success was obviously assisted by changing attitudes in the wider society. During the parliamentary reception that followed the vote in favour of Equal Marriage in the Scottish Parliament, I found myself talking for a few minutes with Jackson Carlaw, a Conservative MP with whom it would be very difficult to imagine any common ground. But common ground there was. We found we both held strongly to the view that it was only right that finally, after so many years, our friends in same-sex relationships could now enjoy the same legal right to marry that we'd been accustomed to as heterosexuals all our lives. Sometimes historical wrongs do get righted. Sometimes progress really happens.

PROLOGUE

It is very important, when looking back over the progress that has been made in Equalities and social inclusion over recent decades, to remember that there is nothing inevitable about progress. The pendulum can always swing back, what is good can always be undone. We have every reason to fear the intentions of well-funded religious extremists, both Christian fundamentalist and Salafist, with their long-term agendas of imposing religious conformity, exterminating LGBTQIA+ people and depriving women of civil rights and bodily autonomy. We must remain watchful and active in supporting human rights for this is a struggle which by its very nature will never be over. I hope and trust that the Scottish PF, under its energetic and extremely capable new leadership, will always stand at the very forefront of this fight.

Blessings

John Macintyre

Scottish Pagan Federation Presiding Officer
2006–2009 & 2015–2018
Pagan Federation President 2008–2010

Foreword

Thomas Lanting

PAGANISM & SEXUALITY – MY JOURNEY

Since adolescence when I, like so many others, started to become aware of who I was, I started to realise that the religion I was born into wasn't something I could connect with. Many people have their own reasons, but for me it was (what I subsequently learnt) the lack of empathy for differences within people that started to lead me down the older paths.

Throughout high school, I was fortunate enough to have two amazing history teachers that, by all accounts, were not dogmatic to the Christian Brothers' curriculum and were very blunt about Christianity's role in the destruction of first peoples, and who allowed us to freely explore topics beyond the church veil.

I found it fascinating to study the structures of Aboriginal, Polynesian and Native American societies and beliefs. It didn't take me long to realise that whatever form my sexuality took, it would have been considered a normal and healthy part of these societies. I will explore these ideas and others in Chapter 9.

Years later, after finding myself travelling through Europe and subsequently making my home in Scotland, I found myself once again exploring sexuality and its role in history.

From great leaders, such as Alexander the Great to amazing people, such as Alan Turing, whose work was pivotal in turning the tide of WWII – an individual's sexuality has historically been used to lessen people's achievements.

As our understanding of sexuality(ies) grows, and with it society's widening acceptance of a range of expression of sexuality, it is hoped that everyone will be able to take their place proudly within the world, no longer confined by the clichés that some people have been tagged with.

I'm Proud to be gay. I'm Proud to be Pagan.

Though these are only two fragments of my identity, they now allow me the privilege of being SPF's first LGBTQIA+ Officer. A role that I, and whoever comes after me, can be proud of holding as we explore the wonders of Paganism via an LGBTQIA+ perspective and help to promote equality within Paganism. The work of this role will not be complete until we reach a point when

FOREWORD

sexuality itself means nothing to anyone and all anyone ever sees is individual value based on humanity.

I hope this book will be a guide and tool, not just to the Pagan LGBTQIA+ community, but to every Pagan. When we see everyone as equal in spirit, and voice, we really can make a difference.

With Love and Light to All

Thomas Lanting

Scottish PF LGBTQIA+ Officer

1

The SPF – Sexuality and Diversity

The Scottish Pagan Federation was established with three principles, which all members are asked to agree and adhere to. These basic ideas drawn up by John Macintyre are fundamental to how Pagans not only work with, but how they understand and respect *all* aspects of society.

The three principles are, however, intended to be a guide, not a doctrine. They are formulated differently from those of PF England and Wales (now no longer used by PFE&W) as SPF's are more in line with those of the Scottish Government and other public sector organisations within Scotland.

As will be discussed in more detail later; in Scotland, SPF is part of the Scottish Interfaith Community and our many celebrants are able to conduct legal Pagan weddings (often referred to as handfastings).

Listed here are SPF's three principles as well as any relevance to LGBTQIA+ culture:

Love for and kinship with Nature. Reverence for the life force and its ever-renewing cycles of life and death.

The first principle emphasises the importance of love and respect for nature in Paganism. It recognises that human beings are part of Nature and that our lives are intimately interwoven with the web of life and death.

In order to hold Nature in love and respect, we have to see it in its dualities. Many species of life have dual natures. Many species are intersex, gay, bi or transgender. Sexual behaviour between both same and opposite members of the same species has been commonly observed in both domesticated and wild animals. If we are truly respecting of *all* that Nature is, and believe that we are fully a part of it, then we must also understand that Nature's sexual expression takes a huge variety of forms.

A positive morality, in which the individual is responsible for the discovery and development of their true nature in harmony with the outer world and community. This is often expressed as: 'Do what you will, as long as it harms none.'

The second principle puts forward a broadly humanistic approach to ethics which seeks to maximise both individual freedom and personal responsibility. It recognises our place as human beings within the web of life and that everything we do, or refrain from doing, has consequences for ourselves and for others. It encourages working towards peaceful outcomes whilst acknowledging the legitimacy of both self-defence and justice.

Taking the first and second principles together, it follows that a truthful harmony with Nature is more likely to be attained if we are willing to see the abundance of varied sexualities as expressed throughout it. Anyone on a Pagan path should hopefully be aiming to understand others' sexualities because, if we can make peace with the idea of sexuality being expressed in a variety of ways in plants, fish, birds and other animals, then we really shouldn't have any issues with this in humanity either.

This is compatible with all Pagan paths and essential for a tolerant, diverse and humane society. The Wiccan Rede is given as an illustrative, but not definitive, example of this general approach to ethics. The Rede does not insist that we harm none under any or all circumstances, but it does encourage us to be aware of the context in which our actions operate, to consider the probable consequences of the choices we make, to make choices that are reasonable and proportionate in the circumstances, to minimise such harm as cannot be prevented, and to take responsibility for our own contribution to the outcome as a result of our action or inaction. Complex ethical decisions are often not so much about whether harm will happen, but about mitigating it.

Paganism is driven by our deep desire to nurture truth in ourselves and in the land, through being respectful to all living creatures. If Pagans are truly seeking to act in accordance with moral codes, such as 'harm none' or 'the rule of three,' then an attitude of nurture will instinctively be part of any Pagan's philosophy.

Recognition of the Divine, which transcends gender, acknowledging both the female and male aspect of Deity.

The third principle encompasses a range of Pagan understandings of divinity including, but not restricted to, pantheism, all forms of polytheism including duotheism, Goddess-recognisant monotheism, and animism. It requires Pagans to acknowledge that where the divine is understood as deity, or deities, who have a gender, then a goddess or goddesses must be included, as well as a god or gods.

This also recognises that there are Pagan understandings of divinity which cannot be categorised by gender. Modern Paganism tends to approach theology through a synergy of multiple understandings of the Divine (or divinity in the abstract) and modern Pagans tend to regard the honouring of the gods (or the Divine as it is manifest within this living world) as of greater importance than theological speculation as to its or their precise nature.

Throughout the world and across time there have been plenty of deities, both gods and goddesses, who are dul aspect, i.e. both male and female. One example is in the Aztec creation stories where *Ometecuhtli* was created and then born of themselves, giving birth in turn to the four gods of the elements.

Innana/Ishtar, as well as many other goddesses, were associated with intersex and trans priestesses. Norse gods commonly changed sex at will; *Loki*, for example, is both the father of *Fenrir* and *Hel*, yet also the mother of *Sleipnir*. The Hindi God of Fire *Agni*, as well as *Mitra* and *Varuna*, also have interesting LGBTQIA+ myths associated with them.

2

The Roots of Sexual Diversity in Ancient World Beliefs

It is, perhaps, particularly important for us, as Pagans, to be striving for sexual equalities to be part of our structure, not just within our beliefs but within society, given the often fluid genders of our deities. LGBTQIA+ beliefs and understanding have been prevalent throughout the world's history; they have not always been considered unnatural or wrong. Such beliefs have helped shape the understanding of creation, as well as being at the epicentre of it.

This chapter seeks to provide a brief summary of some of these beliefs in order to illustrate this argument.

The Australian Aboriginals have a few gender-fluid spirits. The great Rainbow Serpent God *Ungud* is masculine but also seen as feminine. LGBTQIA+ Aboriginals include the blue skinned

Labarinjas who are viewed as women that have both a vagina and a penis.

Among modern Aboriginal communities, transgender people are often called Sistergirls or Brotherboys. Although the Elders within these communities have welcomed them (helping them to return to pre-colonization days), there are still high rates of suicide and discrimination within the general community. 'Black Rainbow' was set up to help LGBTQIA+ Aboriginals and their communities.

In New Zealand, Māori's are also re-embracing their early beliefs. Sexuality was openly expressed in traditional Māori culture, with stories and songs written about all relationships. 'Takatāpui' is a Māori word which describes couples in caring relationships and is embraced within the LGBTQIA+ umbrella.

Within the Pacific Islands, many spirits are seen as both male and female, with a third gender being seen as a norm. The Polynesian Islands have the greatest number of gender-bending deities. Amongst them, Vanuatu's shark-headed god *Qat* approves relationships among males, acting as a guardian of homosexuality.

The Hawaiian goddesses *Wahineomo* and *Hi'iaka* (*Hula*, Magic Goddess) and the human *Hopoa* are all represented as being in relationships together with each other at one time or another. Of these, perhaps the saddest story is of bisexual *Hi'iaka* and her lover *Hopoa*. *Pele*, the Volcano Goddess, killed *Hopoa* with lava as she suspected *Hi'iaka* of having an affair with her husband. Another myth tells of *Pauopalae*, the Fern Goddess, and the goddess *Hi'iaka* together in a lesbian relationship, whilst other stories offer accounts of polyamorous relationships between the deities. Similarly, on the Hawaiian island of Maui, the Pig God *Kamapua* had relationships with the bisexual Sea God *Limaloa*.

In Borneo, *Mahatala-Jata,* is a trans deity who represents the tree; combined with his sister, *Jata*, they symbolise the upper and lower worlds. The God/dess *Menjaya Raja Manang* of Borneo was the chief deity of the transgender shamans: the 'Manang Bali' who were the principal healers.

In the Philippines, it is believed that the trans deity *Bathala* created the universe.

Ancient Sumaria provides much evidence for third gender acceptance. The Supreme God *Enki* requested the Mother Goddess of the Mountains, *Ninmah*, to create them to fulfil the role of priest(ess). Likewise, Mesopotamia's Goddess *Innana's* priests (Gala) were third gender and Babylonia's Goddess *Ishtar* could change her priests' sex to female by supernatural means.

In Egypt, the myth of *Set* and *Horus* and their semen is one of the closest LGBTQIA+ concepts, although the Goddess *Isis* is considered a natural ally and in some stories is seen in a form of relationship with the Scorpion Goddess *Wadjet*, as well her own sister *Nephthys*. The Nile Fertility Gods *Wadj-wer* and *Hapi* are usually depicted with breasts.

Celtic myth was originally oral; today it largely survives in later writings which only reach us after having been filtered by the Christian monks who documented it. Given that these chroniclers almost certainly applied their own censorship, any evidence for LGBTQIA+ behaviour between mythic characters seems to have been removed from the stories. Instead, all we have are glimpses into the Celtic world by ancient Greek and Roman authors who report relationships and handfastings between both sexes and which certainly hint at the practice of polyandry.

Norse culture is similarly filtered; the mythologies being collected by Christian writers. A few stories remain, within the sagas, which suggest that homosexuality was accepted as part of society. Some of the Norse deities, particularly *Loki*, can shapeshift into male and female forms.

Ancient Chinese writings, however, are full of LGBTQIA+ references. From dragons that enjoy having sex with older men, to animal spirits and fairies that choose same-sex human partners. The Rabbit God *Tu Er Shen* is reported as being involved in gay love affairs and relationships in Taoist belief.

In Japan, *Shudō Daimyōjin* is the folk Shinto deity of homosexuality. Whist Ōyamakui is a transgender mountain deity of industry and childbearing.

Although diverse, the indigenous peoples of the Americas share a sense of equality with an acceptance of more than two genders. Traditionally, Native American 'two spirit' people were male, female, and sometimes intersexed individuals who combined activities of both men and women with traits unique to their status. In most tribes, they were considered neither men nor women; they occupied a distinct, alternative gender status. Furthest to the north, Inuit lore tells of how the first human couple were both men; in order to have children, one of them was magically given a vagina. The Marine Goddess *Sedna* was seen in stories as either trans, lesbian or bi. Whilst to the south, the Aztecs revered the Flower God *Xochipilli* as a protector of homosexuality and gay prostitution. Meanwhile, the Mayans revered the God *Chinas* – patron of homosexuality.

Many books have been written about ancient Greece and Rome on the vast and numerous LGBTQIA+ relationships with and between the gods and goddesses in these pantheons.

These are just a small selection of narratives from a scattering of world beliefs. This list is by no means exhaustive, but it hopefully demonstrates that, whatever pantheons or cultures modern Pagans choose to work with, there has often been a place in society for the LGBTQIA+ community. Members of the LGBTQIA+ community have deities especially for their needs, LGBTQIA+ behaviour is recorded in various myths and legends, plus members of the LGBTQIA+ community often have a special place and status in many cultures as shamans and spiritual advisors, because they are viewed as being more closely linked to the gods and goddesses.

It is entirely possible to argue that it was only with the wider adoption of patriarchal monotheism that the status of members of the LGBTQIA+ community was denigrated to the point of persecution. And sadly, for many, this necessarily led to the denial of who they really were.

As our world moves to rebalance male and female roles, it is hoped that we will also start to recognise the importance of all sexualities.

3

Sexuality in Magic

There have been many diverse talks and debates as far as magic and sexuality is concerned. Some have regrettably been stereotypical and even bigoted to the point of stressing that only a straight (cisgender) couple can work at this level, with the god and the goddess being represented by, and invoked into, a male priest and a female priestess.

It would be more inclusive to be open to how sexuality in *all* its forms heightens our own individualities. Our sexuality enshrines us with our own self-worth and centres our very being. When we are fully attuned to ourselves, we can be honest and truthful to the energies around and outside us.

The ways in which sexual behaviours can be utilised within magical acts, are as varied as the ways in which sexuality is expressed throughout humanity. Perhaps it is more helpful to re-envision sex magic as *love* magic?

Many people restrict themselves to thinking about sexual behaviour as acts that are physical and involve (at least) one other person. Thinking more inclusively involves viewing sexual behaviour as ranging from being in an intense moment of spiritual oneness with another, right through to having the experience of being a physical body which belongs to Nature, where intimacy and awareness of the world is just as important as human contact.

Being able to manifest magic from intimacy on *any* and *all* levels is achievable without needing to be concerned about what is 'normal', 'abnormal', 'right' or 'wrong'. Our sexuality is part of the beauty of every human. We exist in our own splendour as unique beings, each worthy of value, all of us fully sentient, with our own personal ways of expressing our sexuality, sensuality and emotions.

Within circle work and ritual practices there doesn't need to be any disagreement over who can or should take on the aspect of the god / lord and goddess / lady. By introducing the practice of both roles being open and obtainable by everyone in a coven, for example, it will both enhance and strengthen the magical growth within a group by introducing equality on many levels. The ability to accept our own yin and yang and stabilise and balance them within ourselves will in turn heighten our own abilities to accept all others.

SEXUALITY IN MAGIC

Magic stems from our understanding of Nature. Our masculine and feminine terms do not have the fixed meanings we have enforced on them ourselves. Nature is always evolving to fill in where needed, whether that be through changing sex or utilizing pheromones.

Although the god and goddess represent yin and yang in energies, we as humans (via our DNA) embody both masculine and feminine traits. To be truly honest to our magic and energy we must learn to embrace taking on both aspects.

By embracing the opposites within ourselves, we can heighten our (as well as our coven's, or any other ritual group's) progression to a higher level.

4

Advances in Sexual Inclusiveness Throughout the SPF's History

As the Scottish Pagan Federation is now a distinct entity, separate from PF England & Wales, and more recently from PF Northern Ireland, it puts the SPF in a unique position.

Unlike the rest of the UK, Scotland (as a whole) has responded positively to its LGBTQIA+ community. The Scottish Government's aims of stamping out intolerance, tackling homophobia and transphobia and so on, has helped the country gain a worldwide recognition as a safe country to visit, as well as a perfect place to get married.

With this in mind, the SPF, as a religious / spiritual body, has led the way in the push for Equal Rights and for marriage equality to be accepted as mainstream in Scotland. This, in turn, has allowed the SPF to press ahead on the rights of LGBTQIA+ within the Pagan community.

Currently, SPF's Council is made up of many people who identify with the LGBTQIA+ community. The SPF appointed a LGBTQIA+ Officer early in 2018, and we are now active on social media with a LGBTQIA+ Facebook page. This aids our community in keeping up to date with their understanding of pressing issues and helps SPF to see and seek ways to better improve our own understandings.

We are aware that mental health issues, as well as social and physical issues, play a part within the LGBTQIA+ community. This is why SPF has also appointed a Disabilities Officer and a Mental Health Officer.

The benefit of creating separate officer roles means that both officers are able to work and provide help on specific related issues. These officers share a great skill set and resources between them; they are able to work together or separately. They are both able to offer impartial advice, direct to appropriate experts, or just provide a friendly shoulder to lean on.

SPF is committed to understanding and keeping up to date with *all* sexualities as humanity evolves and changes. SPF is also committed to making sure everyone has the right to be titled with the noun/pronoun that they choose.

A later chapter will help to clarify terms and nouns/pronouns, not just for our community, but also for the benefit of our friends and allies within the greater Pagan community.

5

Marriage Equality & Interfaith Networking

As John mentioned within the prologue, the SPF was, and still is, one of the main vehicles pushing for equality at all levels in Scotland. SPF's separation from the Pagan Federation of England & Wales has allowed it to have a stronger ability to work within a devolved Scotland, given Scotland's separate legal system.

Though separate entities, the SPF remains close friends and allies with the Pagan Federations of England & Wales and the Pagan Federation of Ireland, sharing experience and knowledge.

In 1996, after years of hard work by John Macintyre, the SPF became a member of the Edinburgh Interfaith Association. Through working alongside other faiths in Scotland, Paganism has gained recognition as an official faith and has since been able to fight for marriage equality, as well as helping to protect Pagans from discrimination, in the same manner as practitioners of other mainstream religions are protected.

After many years of campaigning for equal marriage in Scotland, it finally came into law on the 1st January, 2015, with the first LGBTQIA+ legal handfasting being performed by Louise Park on the 18th January, 2015, for myself and my husband, Iain. This made history, being the first legal LGBTQIA+ Pagan wedding to be celebrated in the UK.

During her time as Presiding Officer, Louise ensured that the SPF became a recognised religious body authorised to nominate celebrants to conduct legal Pagan marriages in Scotland in 2004. Louise is the SPF's Celebrants Coordinator. As of the 1st January, 2021, there are a total of 20 approved SPF celebrants, including myself, who have been nominated by SPF to the National Register of Scotland to perform legal wedding ceremonies for both same and different sex couples.

In 2017, the SPF sponsored and financed the first LGBTQIA+ Interfaith Conference of Faith which had four faith communities in attendance. In 2020, the first LGBTQIA+ Pagan Chaplain was installed at the University of Glasgow.

In the 2021 Scottish census there will be the option to choose 'Pagan' in the question on religion. Previously, Pagans had to choose 'other' and write in 'Pagan'. This new option gives Pagans parity with other religions in Scotland.

Further work remains necessary to ensure that Paganism continues to be treated as a respected integral faith in Scotland. In particular, a programme of education is required to guide some other religious bodies in being less prejudiced against Pagans and Paganism.

6

Twenty Years of Scottish Government and its Impact on Sexuality

Since the formation of the Scottish Parliament in 1997, Scotland has pushed forward with its agenda to overcome inequality within its population. This is in part thanks to The Equality Network which was also set up in the same year. Thus, 1997 marked an important moment where Scotland was able to more directly make decisions for its people.

It is incredible to think that it was only in 1980 that homosexuality was decriminalised in Scotland; this was thirteen years later than in England and Wales.

In 1995, Scotland experienced its first Pride Parade in its capital of Edinburgh. In contrast,

England had had its first in 1972, in London, on the date of the third anniversary of America's Stonewall riots.

A new century has seen the momentum for positive change speed up significantly in Scotland.

In 2000, the Armed Forces lifted their ban on the LGBTQIA+ community within the entire UK, allowing far more people to join the military. This was changed due to the United Nations.

Also in 2000, Section 28 – previously introduced by Margaret Thatcher – which forbade LGBTQIA+ being taught in schools and even prevented libraries from having LGBTQIA+ related material in stock. Although this law has been repealed, it is now becoming an issue again in English schools.

In 2001, the age of consent for LGBTQIA+ individuals was brought into line with the heterosexual age of consent. Although the age of consent in Scotland is 16, England and Wales also changed that year. Northern Ireland changed in 2009.

In 2004, the UK Parliament brought in the Gender Recognition Legislation; this was introduced in order to give gender dysmorphic people the ability to change their gender. This act covers all of the UK.

In 2004, civil partnerships were introduced to allow the LGBTQIA+ community to enter into a legal contract which offered parity with the rights that marriage provided. This was the first step to achieving Equal Marriage rights. However, for many people, civil partnerships were viewed more as business contracts, rather than being associated with love, as marriage contracts are. This is why the LGBTQIA+ community pushed so hard to be allowed to marry: almost is not the same. To further equalise the law, the Scottish Government intends to introduce civil partnerships for opposite, as well as same-sex, couples.

In 2007, two years after it was passed in England and Wales, Scotland passed the Adoption Equality Act. This was extended in 2010 to include trans parents. The act insures all would-be adoptive parents are assessed fairly without being subject to religious (or other) prejudice.

The Discrimination in Services Act was brought into motion in 2006–7 throughout the UK and extended in 2010 to ensure everyone has the right to public services without persecution or discrimination.

In 2008, the Equality in Fertility Law was introduced.

Hate crime laws were reinforced in 2009, including protecting the LGBTQIA+ community. These provisions are constantly adapting as needs arise.

In 2010, the Equality Act was broadened so that people from every area in the UK, apart from Northern Ireland, have the same protection of LGBTQIA+ rights.

The Equal Marriage Act was final passed in Scotland in January 2014, a few months after being introduced in England. Northern Ireland finally caught up on the 13th January, 2020.

Please note, as the Scottish Pagan Federation has been recognised as a body suitable to approve celebrants by the Registrar General for Scotland since 2004, Scotland was the first country in the UK to actually celebrate a LGBTQIA+ Pagan marriage. In England and Wales, it is still not possible to have a legal Pagan wedding.

The Scottish Government is currently exploring ways of improving equality for the trans community.

7
Sexuality & Discrimination

As we reflect upon our current understanding of sexuality, both in its myriad of forms as well as its personal effects upon an individual's interpretation of themselves and their world, I would like to highlight something that seems to connect us as a species: we tend to naturally judge and discriminate.

Our tendency to discriminate as a collective may be a natural character trait, inherited from our ancestors, or it might be something we only do unconsciously. For example, we have an apparently inbuilt animal desire to find the best mate, and our choices are affected by physical appearance or psychological factors. It seems to be a natural part of our evolution, but does that make it morally right?

We all know people who would *never* think of being in a relationship with someone based on a decision about their (dis)ability, age, or ethnic origin, for example. Likewise, when we observe relationships which seem to contravene our own prejudices, we might consciously or subconsciously make assessments of that couple.

For example, stereotypical male/female ideals in which an older man with a younger female will get a congratulatory response from most straight men. Conversely, an older female with a younger male tends to elicit a more negative response.

If we take the time to reflect on it, in a painful and honest manner, most of us will discover that we hold discriminative opinions when viewing others. These can derive from old stereotypes, fears, insecurities and even underlying jealousies. And although we might scoff at age differences within relationships, we generally don't view it in the same way as we view an able-bodied person being in a relationship with someone disabled. Personally, I have witnessed someone saying (of a differently-abled couple): 'Oh that's sweet how close they are to their carer,' and even: 'if you lost a limb we'd have to divorce.' Even if such things are said as an automatic reaction or as a joke, it places an immediate fear into the relationship that we can't rely on our loved one.

Within the LGBTQIA+ community, discrimination can be particularly ferocious. This has to do with social background and family support. If

SEXUALITY & DISCRIMINATION

a child grows up knowing his/her/their sexuality and only hearing their loved ones speaking with fear, hatred or disgust about certain sexualities, then they will either fiercely rebel and separate from that environment as soon as they are able to, or start believing that they are disgusting in themselves, bringing on depression, bullying of other LGBTQIA+ youth or – worse – commit suicide.

We create how our children see themselves and their world. Don't be the parent who loses a child to prejudice. What *you* do has a great effect on their future.

Within both the gay and lesbian community, discrimination can be segmented and what has been learned from our parents/wider family/social environment becomes magnified. People that act overtly feminine or butch can be subjugated to being made a joke of, mocked, and even seen as an embarrassment.

We now live in a society that can be overtly superficial, where we are encouraged to sideline someone who doesn't fit our 'selfie' society. If we can't edit it or airbrush it, it doesn't fit. Yet, despite all of this, and perhaps as a result of advertisements and social media, we are starting to see a wider range of society being presented both onscreen and online. Certainly, those people are still preened and even airbrushed, but there is some hope that, now we are able to see other people as people, rather than just as their disabilities, we might also start to be more socially aware of everyone's need to be seen, to be loved, and to be valued as equal.

One of the biggest causes of death within the LGBTQIA+ community has long been, and continues to be suicide, due to mental health issues. For many young people, bullying can be a norm but, unlike a cisgender child, teachers generally tend to ignore it for a LGBTQIA+ child or even tell them, in a manner of words, that they deserve it.

Today many schools are becoming better equipped to tackle this problem, however, a recent poll by the BBC found that being LGBTQIA+ is still the main reason given for bullying, at 13% of cases. This compares to bullying on the grounds of ethnicity, at 11%.

The need to tackle these issues today is a major way of helping the community of the future, not just mentally but also physically.

The most recent research on the LGBTQIA+ community is well worth a read to help shed light on the focus needed for mental health and wellbeing within our community: https://www.gov.uk/government/publications/national-lgbt-survey-summary-report/national-lgbt-survey-summary-report#the-results

An emerging global issue, particularly within Christian countries, is the practice of gay conversion therapy. This cruel and insensitive practice (via prayer, electroshock therapy, chemical castration, etc.) has resulted in many LGBTQIA+ youths running away from home at a young age. Although it has been dispelled by almost every modern health board as inhuman, the practice still continues. In the UK, the government has yet to make the practice illegal. All British health boards, as well as many religious leaders, have denounced the practice.

As is the case for all discrimination, it's important to reiterate that the way in which people are treated by their family and faith community (as well as their friends) at an early age can have a long-term impact on how people associate with their own sexualities, intimacies and inner belief in their own unique being. When people start to resent that which is normal and natural to them, it can escalate to destroy their own mental health.

A major way we can all support the LGBTQIA+ community is to accept and understand their feelings and realise that our actions and words can have a massive impact on another's mental health. As Pagans, we have a unique capacity to be inclusive and to contribute towards making our LGBTQIA+ community members feel secure and part of a healthy spiritual environment.

Here follows some suggestions for improving inclusive practice with Paganism:

1. Understanding our own deities' multiple sexualities and being minded that their singular sexual identities may have been a relatively modern change imposed by Christian interpretations of those documenting them (for example, early medieval monks).
2. Choose to call a person by their chosen identity; for someone who is struggling to be seen as the person inside, this courtesy can mean the world.
3. In ritual practice, allow any roles (particularly gendered roles such as that of lord and lady) to be explored by *all* members of the working group. Apart from giving a clear message that everyone is accepted, this is a powerful way for (cisgender) males and females to take in and work with their own sacred dual self.
4. Within moots, explore the role of sexuality within Paganism and the roles acceptance and understanding have in magic. This could be an interesting discussion topic.

5. Teach our children that *all* sexualities and *all* humans matter. If we can promote the message of universal love, yet ignore the rights of others, then we fail at the very core of magic. All are equal. There is a true purpose for everything. Perfect balance = perfect trust.

In the current circumstances, where even today 1 in 7 LGBTQIA+ people still feel unable to disclose their sexuality openly to a trained medical professional, it is clear there is still a lot of work needed to be done for the LGBTQIA+ community to feel safe and secure about living their lives in the manner which a cisgender person takes for granted.

For example, when it comes to sexual health, the LGBTQIA+ community have been highly stigmatised and even demonised as 'dirty'. This was a key emotional trigger for the guilt-inducing and traumatic AIDS government advice disseminated in the 1980s: 'Don't Die of Ignorance.' HIV / AIDS has for many (especially for the older generations) been their main context of what happens outside of social norm (i.e. straight) sexual relations.

Instead, and thanks to official data from the NHS and the Terrance Higgins Trust, we can hopefully try to change these misconceptions and recognise that sexual health is important for people of all sexualities. Using 2019 official records for the UK as a whole, there were 105,200 people living with HIV, out of whom only 41% were LGBTQIA+. Today, 97% of people with HIV (thanks to modern drugs) have an undetectable viral load (it cannot be passed on) and a full lifespan is normal.

As already discussed, sexual health and mental health impact on each other; many people who do not feel loved, or who feel that they don't belong, will instinctively try to reach out for physical interaction. What the health records of the UK reveal is that since general acceptance of the LGBTQIA+ community has been written into law and a certain degree of normalisation has taken place (for example, marriage and adoption rights for gay couples, etc.), the rate of sexual infection has actually reduced significantly. Clearly, treating everyone as equal has many benefits for the whole of society.

8

Sexuality & Mental Health

Mental health is a major stigma that the majority of LGBTQIA+ people live with. For many, this can start from childhood within an intolerant family, followed by years of bullying at school.

In current circumstances, where even today 1 in 7 feel the need to not disclose openly to a trained medical professional, it shows there is still a lot of work needed to be done for the community to feel safe and secure about living their lives just as a cis person does.

Within the SPF there is a dedicated Mental Health Officer. As I was writing this book, I realised I wanted to have someone who has a degree in mental health to be the voice of this chapter. It is my hope that this can be a source of help and a guide, should you need it.

Mental Health & Well-being Officer

Matt Cormack

MBACP is a person-centred counsellor and a registered member of the British Association for Counselling and Psychotherapy. He is the Mental Health and Well-being Officer for the Scottish Pagan Federation.

This chapter intends to offer a brief introduction into mental health within the context of LGBTQIA+ people. It will look at five areas: mental health, suicide, conversion therapy, accessing services and looking after your mental health. It is crucial to note that nothing in this chapter is to be taken as medical advice, nor is anything mentioned here a substitute or replacement for medical treatment. If you have concerns about your mental or physical heath, please consult your primary healthcare provider.

MENTAL HEALTH AND LGBTQIA+ PEOPLE

Anyone can experience mental health issues and everyone's mental health matters. When we look at issues that can lead to issues such as depression and anxiety, LGBTQIA+ people are at higher risk of experiencing mental health issues.

Many LGBTQIA+ people can feel isolated, particularly if they are in a small community without many other LGBTQIA+ people with whom they can connect with. Whilst this is improving, as acceptance of different sexualities increases and internet access widens, it still affects the community. Rejection can affect LGBTQIA+ people's mental health. Coming out can be frightening and distressing for some because there are fears they may be rejected by the people they tell. Lack of visibility can also have an effect on the mental health of LGBTQIA+ people; however, this is improving over time.

Stigma, homophobia and transphobia have a huge impact on LGBTQIA+ people's mental health. For some, there can be a constant anxiety of being targeted or attacked for being who they are. Many LGBTQIA+ people have reported being the victim of a hate crime; 1,216 hate crimes relating to sexual orientation and trans identity were reported in Scotland between 2018–2019. However, this does not tell us how many people were victims of hate crimes and did not report it.

We know from research that LGBTQIA+ people experience a higher proportion of mental illness than the rest of the population. Stonewall's report of LGBTQIA+ people in Britain shows that 52% of LGBTQIA+ people have experienced depression in the last year. These numbers are even higher, as 67% of trans people had experienced depression. The report also shows us that LGBTQIA+ people who have suffered a hate crime have higher rates of depression. Finally, it is important to note that intersectionality plays a role with LGBTQIA+ people's experience of depression, as we see higher rates of depression among LGBTQIA+ people of colour (62%) and people from low-income households (64%). 61% of LGBTQIA+ people reported experiencing anxiety in the same report.

The person-centred approach suggests that we have an organismic self, which is who we really are. We also have a self-concept which is who we try to be or feel we must be. If these two are significantly different then it can lead to distress. Introjected values are values we hold but have come from others around us, such as family or religion – so, internalised homophobia or transphobia could be an introjected value. A condition of worth is when we feel we must do something or behave in a certain way to be accepted or receive love. A parent only willing to love their child if they are not LGBTQIA+ could be a condition of worth. Both introjected values and conditions of worth can cause a person to attempt to be different to whom they actually are, which can cause them distress.

SUICIDE

Suicide affects the LGBTQIA+ community substantially. Research into LGBTQIA+ people shows that suicidal thoughts are higher than in the rest of the population with 44% of LGBTQIA+ young people having reported thoughts of suicide and 50% having self-harmed at some point in their life. Three years later, Stonewall reported that 13% of LGBTQIA+ people aged 18–24 had attempted suicide and 52% had suicidal thoughts. This strongly suggests that suicide continues to be one of the biggest issues LGBTQIA+ people face.

There are a lot of ways to get support if you are struggling with thoughts of harming yourself or suicide. Speaking to your GP can be helpful; they are trained and can support you if you have any of these thoughts. It can also help to talk to someone you trust, such as a friend, partner, or family member. There are numbers and websites in the 'Health & Well-being' section in the appendix if you need to speak to someone.

WHAT IS CONVERSION THERAPY?

Conversion or cure or reparative therapy refers to a number of practices which attempt to change the sexuality or gender identity of a person. It has been shown to be harmful and unethical. It has also been shown to be ineffective: it does not 'work'. There is research showing that people who have experienced this therapy can be twice as likely to have thought about or attempted suicide. In the LGBTQIA+ 'Health in Britain' report we see that 1 in 20 people have been pushed towards questioning or changing their sexuality or gender identity when trying to access healthcare services. Conversion therapy is not currently illegal in the UK, although there are people calling for it to be made illegal.

The British Association for Counselling and Psychotherapy (BACP) explicitly says in their ethical framework that counsellors and psychotherapists should not try to change someone's sexuality or gender identity:

> 'Challenge assumptions that any sexual orientation or gender identity is inherently preferable to any other and will not attempt to bring about a change of sexual orientation or gender identity or seek to suppress an

individual's expression of sexual orientation or gender identity.'

BACP Ethical Framework Point 22e

While BACP is only one therapist membership body amongst many, no therapist should attempt to change a client's sexual or gender identity. If a person feels their therapist is trying to do this, they can challenge them or make a complaint to that therapist's membership body. Counselling and Psychotherapy in Scotland (COSCA) Statement of Ethics and Code of Practice sections 2.5 and 2.6 talk about respecting and recognising diversity. The British Psychological Society (BPS) Code of Ethics and Conduct section 3.1 talks about treating clients with respect.

ACCESSING MENTAL HEALTH SERVICES

Accessing mental health services can be difficult for some LGBTQIA+ people, particularly people who are not out. This section is trying to let you know some of your rights when accessing mental health services, where you can get more information, and how to find services near you. The information here will be focused on Scotland, there will necessarily be different provision in other countries.

You have a right to be treated fairly and you should not be discriminated against for being LGBTQIA+. As was mentioned in the section about conversion therapy, no one should be trying to change your sexuality or gender identity when you access services for mental health.

Speaking with professionals should be confidential, meaning that what you say to them should not be discussed with family or others. There are some circumstances where it is required to break confidentiality, such as suicide risk, but you should be informed of this.

In the NHS, you may see staff wearing rainbow lanyards or badges. These were created so that LGBTQIA+ people would know that this is a safe person to be open with.

Counselling is available through the NHS, although there are often long waiting lists. Many charities offer free or low-cost therapy, and it is worth contacting some to find out if they can help. Some people decide to access private therapy.

One important thing to note here is that 'counsellor', 'therapist' and 'psychotherapist' are not protected titles. This means that anyone can call themselves a therapist with no training. It is always worth asking what qualifications or training someone has.

Counselling and psychotherapy membership bodies have ethical frameworks their members must abide by. They have minimum training standards to be able to join and have a complaints process for clients who wish to raise a complaint. Most of these membership bodies are members of the Professional Standards Authority (PSA). It is worth asking a potential therapist if they are a member of one of these bodies. Five of the main ones are Counselling and Psychotherapy in Scotland (COSCA), British Association for Counselling and Psychotherapy (BACP), British Psychological Society (BPS), National Counselling Society (NCS) and UK Council for Psychotherapy (UKCP).

If you are looking to find a therapist then there are several places you can look. Two of the main websites are Counselling Directory and Psychology Today. Most of the membership bodies previously mentioned have directories of their own members you can search. There is also the Pink Therapy network where you can find therapists who are aware of LGBTQIA+ issues.

TIPS FOR FINDING A THERAPIST:

- Search on directory or membership body websites for potential therapists.

- Find out about their qualifications, training and if they are registered with a membership body.
- Check their costs.
- Find out what kind of therapy they offer, modalities of counselling can be vastly different!
- You can call or email a potential counsellor with any questions.
- Some counsellors offer a free session to see if you can work together. This is a chance to see how you work together and ask questions.
- If you feel a particular therapist isn't the right fit for you then that is ok, you don't have to stay with them and there are others you can get in touch with.

LOOKING AFTER YOUR MENTAL HEALTH

For many people, medication or therapy are ways of maintaining their mental health. Each person is unique, so different medications or therapies might work better for some than for others. These are good subjects to discuss with your GP.

Spiritual practice can be a part of maintaining our mental health, as an important aspect of self-care. Many Pagan practices involve some personal reflection and introspection, which can help people to be curious about how they are feeling. Similarly, going outside and connecting with Nature can be helpful for some people. Some people might use everyday activities as part of their spiritual practice for supporting their mental health. Blessing the water from your shower to cleanse you or stirring intentions for the day into a cup of tea are small ways to unite spirituality and self-care.

Rituals can play a big part in our mental health; we can perform rituals for almost anything. A ritual calling on a deity to support you during a difficult time can bring comfort, or perhaps you can light a candle to remember someone who has died. Worden's theory of grief teaches that rituals as a part of acknowledging loss are essential for the four tasks of mourning.

A common practice within the Pagan community is meditation. There are several different types of meditation which work for different people. There are many websites, apps and videos which offer information about meditation and you can find guided meditations online. While meditation can be helpful for many people, not everyone finds it helpful.

Bessel Van Der Kolk speaks about the efficacy of yoga as a part of looking after mental health and processing trauma. Yoga can be a way to connect with the physical body in a way that enables a person to notice their body without becoming overwhelmed.

We are all unique, with our own individual needs. Looking after your mental health may be different to those around you – and that is ok. Find ways that work for you, be curious about yourself and know that there are many people you can speak to if you need support.

9
An A-Z Understanding of Sexuality – Scientific & Medical Descriptions

The meanings of several terms that describe sexuality have been listed in many dictionaries as well as on-line. Although they have no emotional connection attached to them, they *are* necessarily laden with subtle and often loaded meanings for many people who are trying to understand their fellow humans. Some terms are still, sadly, used in an insulting manner. In a world where we are developing our sexual identities ever more, this list is not intended to be a static one but rather it will grow as society's understanding of its sexual selves likewise grows.

Aromantic – A person with no desire for a romantic relationship.

Asexual – A person without sexual feelings one way or the other.

Bisexual – A person who loves and can have a sexual relationship with either sex.

Cisgender – Relates to anyone who perceives their personal identity and sexuality to be associated with the gender allocated to them at birth, i.e. a man assigned to a man's body. Opposite of transgender.

Drag – A person who dresses up to entertain.

Gay – A word used to describe male homosexual culture as well as a man who loves and/or has sex with men.

Gender-fluid – A person who doesn't see themselves as a fixed gender.

Intersex – A person who has both male and female sexual characteristics or body parts. A person inbetween traditional concepts.

Lesbian – A woman who loves women and/or has sexual relationships with women.

Non-binary – A person who is more androgynous in gender and sexuality.

Omnisexual – An individual who is attracted to persons of all genders and orientations. The term is often used as a synonym for pansexual.

Panromantic – A person who is romantically attracted to people of all sexual orientations and gender identities.

Pansexual – A person who, whilst in a relationship, doesn't consider gender identity, biological sex or gender.

Polyamorous – A person who can be in many different sexual relations at the same time, all of which are consensual.

Queer – The American group Queer Nation introduced this as an umbrella term for all LGBTQIA+ people but please note that some people still consider this to be a derogatory word and, for this reason, it is best to check that the person to whom it is being applied is accepting of its application before using it.

Sapiosexual – A person who finds intelligence sexually attractive or arousing.

Straight – A person who only has relations with the opposite sex to them.

Tomboy – A girl who exhibits characteristics or behaviours considered typical of a boy; for example, wearing masculine clothing, preferring more physical games and interests.

Trans female – Allocated as male at birth, but identifying as female.

Transgender – A person who does not consider their sexuality and their birth body as compatible.

Trans male – Allocated as female at birth, but identifying as male.

Transsexual – A person who considers that they belong to the opposite sex, both psychologically and emotionally (this term is going out of use; traditionally this term was applied after surgery). This term is more likely to be used by older people, as a reference for themselves, to describe the medical change to their true self.

Transvestite/Cross-dresser – A person who enjoys wearing clothes more usually associated with the opposite sex.

10

An A-Z Understanding of Sexuality Through the Eyes of the LGBTQIA+ Community

An entry in a dictionary can only ever offer a limited and descriptive explanation of a word that is being used to communicate an emotion or aspect of sexuality; it cannot convey a definitive account that also fully covers all the nuances of the feelings associated with the word.

Members of the LGBTQIA+ community were asked to provide their own meanings and understanding of some of these terms. It is hoped that these more personal responses will provide a better understanding of the human aspect of each term.

Within the many responses received, I had a difficult time deciding which ones to use as, on many, I was lucky to have four or five to choose from. I'm thankful to everyone within the LGBTQIA+ community who chose to respond and make this section possible.

Aromantic – 'I've never felt that romantic spark with anyone. In a relationship, I've never felt the desire to be lovey, hold hands, etc. I can still have a loving relationship with someone that others might see as platonic but that context isn't there.'

Asexual – 'For me, there are feelings of sensuality but these do not arise from other people. I feel that sex is a mechanical act, whereas sensuality comes from my relationships with the natural world around me. My Paganism is rooted in the heart, in plants and trees. An unfurling leaf is sensual in texture, shape and smell; shells and stones have a power to move me deeply. I have never felt the same with a human being.'

Bisexual – 'To me, I think I fall into the bisexual category. I love women as much as I love men. The difference for me is that, if I'm in a relationship, I stay within the boundaries of our relationship;

meaning, if I'm dating a man, I am with him only and if I am with a woman, I stay with that woman. In my eyes, I am open to love in all forms.'

Cisgender – 'I am a male born in a male body and I'm happy and comfortable in the body I'm in.'

Drag – 'I use drag as an entertainment, to over-emphasise aspects of myself, create a character, and be able to do and say things I would never have the confidence to do in my day-to-day life.'

Gay – 'I realised I was sexually attracted to men quite early, so I have never thought of females in the same way. Being in a same-sex relationship is just natural to me; I never thought of it as anything else.'

Gender-fluid – 'I feel a bit of a shapeshifter. Though, in my case it tends to be a more gradual build up. I can relate as he/him for months then slowly morph as more she/her. I don't personally fully change how I dress but I allow flexibility in my broad wardrobe. I know a few friends who like to really dress how they feel but I'm not comfortable enough for that.'

Intersex – 'Though I was born a boy, I've never really fitted into that role. As a teenager, I really struggled to identify with anyone, as I would be bullied about my feminine features and mannerisms. There was a time where I thought about transitioning, feeling that physically being female would be better all-round but I've grown to accept and understand ME on ALL terms. I am straight. I am effeminate, but my DNA is what it is.'

Lesbian – *(this response is from a couple, hence why the quote is written both in singular and plural)* 'To me, being a lesbian means that I am a woman who loves a woman. I love a woman who looks like a woman. If I wanted to date someone who looked like a man, I would date a man! But I get that we all find different people and looks attractive. I can appreciate a good-looking man but wouldn't feel a physical attraction in the same way. We often say: "I'd stand him in the corner to look at!" The good thing is that, as we both find women attractive, we can acknowledge our appreciation of them without getting in trouble with the other! We are both secure in our relationship and love for one another. Being in a lesbian relationship doesn't mean there has to be a "butch" one! We both possess quite a lot of men's clothes – but this is mostly because we like the styles and in fact it's mostly women who ask me where I got them. I like to think I wear them in a womanly way. I don't try to look like a man.

We both have long hair. I wear it up, down or half and half. We rarely wear makeup but I might do if I'm going out somewhere. I don't like the word lesbian. I don't really know why – I just don't like the sound of it. I will often use gay as a generic term if I need to use a label. I tend not to use labels anyway – if someone asks if I'm gay then I say: "No, I'm (name)!" Or, in conversation, I may refer to my wife – and expand on that if I need to. I see people as just the name they use and who they are ... not an age, gender, sexuality, etc. To be honest, those things don't really go through my mind when I meet or interact with someone.'

Non-binary – 'A lot of people think that being non-binary is about rejecting the concept of gender. I don't see it that way. For me, being non-binary is about embracing all of the spectrum of gender. I don't specifically identify as male or female, and I do not think that either really applies to me, because I feel like I have stepped back and can see both as two halves of the same whole. I can recognise aspects of what people might traditionally label as "male" and "female" within myself, but I do so in the knowledge that these aspects are not separate or opposed to one another. They are all parts of the same whole. I might have a day of wearing sparkly jewellery and baking cakes, but I am still not "female" on those days. Similarly, when I wear "masculine" clothing, I am still not "male". I am all genders.'

Omnisexual – 'I've just always been drawn to who I'm drawn to. I am happily aware of my individual partner's identities but I've never seen that as a hindrance. I see each of my experiences for the sexuality and person they are.'

Panromantic – 'I can experience both romantic attraction and sexual attraction with someone, regardless of their gender. Some folks like to split between the two aspects.'

Pansexual – 'To me, being pansexual means being attracted to people, regardless of their gender. And, to me, that fits with my experiences and how I feel. It does not mean that I'm likely to be unfaithful with anyone who walks by, and it does not mean I love my husband any less because I can experience attraction to a wider range of people than he can.'

Polyamorous – 'Polyamory in summary is a term for ethical non-monogamy where you can love more than one person at the same time. Not all connections will be the same but consent is the key to it being ethical. All parties consent and have knowledge of other partners. How this is expressed depends on the individuals.

Some people have a closed triad and may even live together. I personally identify as solo polyamorous, as I chose not to go down the traditional route of relationships and chose not to live with a partner or get married. This could change in the future but currently I have one partner in Scotland who I see every week and chat with on the phone, and a long-distance partner who lives in Devon and we try to see each other every few months. All our relationships are open to others too. Also, how we interact with what is called a metamour (meaning friendship with your partner's partner) depends on the individuals.'

Queer – *(what follows is a variety of both pro and negative responses to try to communicate the vast differences that exist regarding the use of this term)*

'Growing up, "queer" was not a term I was abused with, so I realise that I lack a certain emotional response associated with its use.'

'For me, queerness encompasses my sexual identity as someone uncomfortable with binary presentation. It also encompasses my rebuke of cisgender and heteronormative privilege. LGBTQIA+ labels tend to presume a binary origination, and their usage coincides with a social movement that seeks assimilation and erases the existence of non-binary identities.

Using "queer" as a catch-all umbrella term, whether intentionally or not, silences that important fringe voice.'

'I loathe the word with every fibre. As, from a child through till the end of university, that term made my life hell. Constantly picked out, yelled across the field at me. It got to the point that if something came on the TV with the title 'Queer', I turned the channel off. The word holds every memory of pain, fear, hurt and sorrow I grew up with.'

'I realise that the word is being "empowered" in a different way but a word of hate will always be a word of hate to a vast swathe of the community.'

Sapiosexual – 'I can happily say that I am attracted to people based more on their personality and intelligence – which takes many forms, it's not just academic intelligence.'

Straight – 'I'm a cisgender woman who has only ever fancied men. I'm not attracted to all males, I'm really rather specific in my tastes, but women just don't do anything for me.'

Tomboy – 'In my opinion, "tomboy" is a word for a female whose interests defy outdated gender norms, whether it's hobbies, interests, professions, or anything like that. I don't think anyone under a certain age is called a "tomboy" anymore because those "boys must do this and girls must do that" days are behind us.'

Trans female – 'Even as a child, I never thought of myself as a boy. I was always happiest playing with my female neighbours and friends than with boys. I tried to hide within my born body at school being sporty but hiding brought on severe depression. After leaving school, I finally took the step to become a female through hormone therapy and surgery. I am now living how I always knew I was. The person who I see in the mirror is the lady that has always been inside.'

Transgender – 'I was born a male and never felt whole. During my 20's and 30's, I would dress up in female clothes and became friends with transvestites, wondering if this was the answer. I realised in a short period of time that this was still not being true to me. Dressing up was just that. I was feeling like it was putting a band aid over a cut. It did, however, help me realise to be true to myself, that I needed to transition and become a full female. I've been a female now for 20 years and have never felt more complete and content within myself.'

Trans male – 'For me, the transition from a female body to a male body has meant becoming my authentic self. Having been born in 1958, I had no knowledge, no access and no support in finding out why I felt "off" in myself. Moving to Europe enabled me to learn how I could join my inner and outer selves to finally become whole. What an amazing feeling! It saved my sanity!'

Transsexual – 'Being transsexual, in my eyes, is knowing from very early on that you were born in the wrong (gender-wise) body. Thinking patterns and preferences also usually follow the brain's idea of said trans person's gender. It's funny actually, because while I'm definitely trans male, I'm most definitely bi. I appreciate beauty and intellect, no matter what package it comes in.'

Transvestite/Cross-dresser – 'Being able to dress up on a night out, or to go out dressed, isn't about believing I'm born the wrong sex, but more to experience life as my partner's sex, as well as gaining a sense of freedom from being someone else.'

11

Nouns & Pronouns – Why are they Important?

This is a subject that will no doubt become more prominent within society in general, as it's not an issue solely reserved to the LGBTQIA+ community but rather one which is constant and evolving, and which involves everyone.

For example, historically 'Miss' or 'Mistress', 'Madam' or 'Ma'am', were terms used to denote female marital and social status. These terms were used to indicate whether a woman was married, a 'spinster', single, young or old.

Being referred to by the appropriate term is important for everyone. It confers respect upon a person and helps people to understand each other. As a society, we are already used to titles such as Mr, Mrs, Sir and Madam. These titles are traditionally used as a way of demonstrating politeness to the individual. In the twenty-first century, we are adapting, through our developed understanding of sexual values, to add to the range of potential titles, in order to provide similar levels of courtesy to everyone.

Today, mainly due to celebrities within the media, society is increasingly becoming aware of how the titles we use for people can adversely affect their overall mental health and self-belief.

Below are some modern examples of titles. Some of these will be familiar but others may be new:

Man	He/Him	
Woman	She/Her	
Gender-neutral	They/Themselves	Yo/Yoself
	Per/Perself	

They / Them / Theirs

- ze (zhee)/zer (zhere)/zers (zheres)
- ze (zhee)/hir (here)/hirs (heres)
- xe (zhee)/xem (zhem)/xyrs (zheres)

American terms added as they may become used in UK later.

When referring to someone's gender, it's important to ask the individual which term they prefer, rather than making an assumption. If you are not sure which to use, it is never rude to ask. Asking politely both respects the person and demonstrates that you value them. As an example, which most of us will be familiar with:

not all females like being called 'Miss', 'Ma'am' or 'Madam'; not all males like being called 'Sir' or 'Mr'.

REMEMBER: If you're not sure, just ask. Manners are free and asking is respecting.

12
Why we Need Allies & How to be One

Having allies is important in all communities. This is especially the case within the LGBTQIA+ community, and some parts of this community desperately need more.

A recent trend witnessed globally in both the cisgender and straight community has seen beautiful demonstrations of support from parents being present to give hugs and show love to anyone in the marches who needs it. This is welcomed on so many levels, particularly by anyone who has been rejected by their family and friends as a consequence of coming out as non-cisgender or non-straight.

As society progresses and more parts of the LGBTQIA+ community become accepted, there will necessarily be dynamic changes which occur within society. Sometimes, even within our communities, we can forget to show support through misunderstanding or other reasons. Currently, this is true for trans and bi members.

If you have family members or friends that are LGBTQIA+, or you just want to show support generally, there are a great many ways that you can become an ally:

- You could take part in the cuddle movement, as described above, or volunteer to fill the parental role at a wedding for someone whose parents don't support them.

- The next time your town has a Pride Parade, go along to show support. Wave a Pride flag, wear a Pride t-shirt, hold a support banner in the air. Pride Parades (at least in the UK) aren't a political march demonstration anymore; they are a celebration of life, struggle and a show of resilience: they are a chance to show that WE are PROUD to be who we are. By showing support as an individual, you not only demonstrate community support, but you may be the person who changes someone else's mind or gives strength to someone in our community who has been ignored / bullied by family, ex-friends and so on.

- As described previously, it is always courteous to ask someone what they prefer to be called.

It not only shows that you care but that you actually are interested in their life.

- If you run a business, or work in retail, ask the manager how you can show support for the community. Sometimes just a Pride / trans / bi triangle/flag decoration or logo in a window can show not just support but lead to others showing support also. The more people in general become accustomed to companies and small shops showing respect and supportive attitudes, the more society will change.

- Don't be afraid to stand up for someone who is being bullied in the workplace, on-line and so on.

- If you have a local LGBTQIA+ community space or youth centre, pop down and see how you can help, for example with fundraising, printing, etc. Many of our community / mental health spaces don't get the help they need and will be grateful for your offer.

- As a parent, there is a stronger need to listen and just be there for your child. Learn the signs of bullying. Check with the school that you will send your child to on literature used. Are they using the latest information on LGBTQIA+ awareness available to teachers? If not, push for it to be addressed and used.

- As a (grand) parent you have the most amazing ability to teach your child(ren) about equality and diversity. It's never too early to teach kindness, respect and love to everyone, regardless of age, sexuality, colour or belief.

13
LGBTQIA+ Deities

This chapter is a reference point for those who wish to work with deities from around the world who are understood as protecting and helping the LGBTQIA+ community, as well as having LGBTQIA+ relationships.

Alongside their names are their countries of origin.

I have incorporated, in the reference section, some starting points for further reading.

Aphrodite – Greece
Although not a lesbian herself, many homoerotic tales were attributed to her. She was referred to by the Greek poet, Sappho, of the island of Lesbos, as the greatest ally of homosexuals and lesbians.

Apollo – Greece
The Greek Sun God and twin brother to Artemis is written to have taken many lovers, both divine and mortal. One story is of Apollo and the beautiful Spartan prince, Hyakinthos.

Ardhanarishvara – India
In Hindu myth, when Parvati and Shiva interconnected their bodies they took on this androgynous form. Split right down the centre, their bond signifies the balance of Nature and knowledge. Worshiped by many trans/non-binary and gender-fluid devotees in India and Bangladesh.

Artemis – Greece
This goddess of youth and the hunt was worshiped by lesbians. Her sexuality can be seen alluded to in her desire to never find a male lover, the love of her female companions and devotees, as well as in the story of Artemis and Calypso.

Athena – Greece
Athena was very different to her fellow deities on Olympus. Unlike most of her kin, Athena mainly kept to herself. Yes, she did have relations but in history and from art she's most known by being with beautiful young maidens, giving rise to the belief she may have been lesbian. However, due to her lack of sexual dalliances we would see her as asexual.

Atum – Egypt
The first of all deities in Egypt was Atum. Like many original deities, they are of both sexes.

Through their own semen or a sneeze (debatable) they gave birth to two children: Shu & Tefnut.

Bahuchara Mata – India
Today in India and Bangladesh, this goddess of chastity and fertility is seen as the protector of the Hijra (eunuchs, trans & intersex) community. Many of the stories of this goddess display evidence of sexual interchange.

Dionysus / Bacchus – Greece
Deity of all things enjoyable and insatiable desires, this god of orgies and the good life was either poly or omnisexual.

Hapi – Egypt
An intersex deity of the Nile. In most depictions of Hapi, they are shown with a male body with breasts, a pregnant belly, a beard and a penis.

Hecate – Southwest Asia Minor and Greece
As a guardian, a keeper of light and protector of the lost, this goddess has entered the hearts of the LGBTQIA+ community. As a goddess between worlds, there is a natural attraction in which we find a kindred guide and mother.

Hermaphroditus – Greece
The story of Hermaphroditus, the child of Aphrodite and Hermes, is an interesting early

account to understand intersex people, as well as children born with both genes. It was the nymph Salmacis' plea to the gods to be forever part of the youth that caused the two becoming one. As a modern take, the story can be seen as a youth developing understanding of their own sexuality.

Ishtar / Inanna – Babylon and Mesopotamia
This sacred deity of Mesopotamia and Sumaria has many fascinating hymns and scripts relating to her which reveal a culture that had a great gender-fluid / trans understanding. Ishtar later became a popular goddess in Egypt under the name Asteroth, or the more Hellenized Astarte. Although they shared many traits and diverged in others, she can be seen depicted as androgynous.

Isis – Egypt
As a mother goddess and protector of the downtrodden, Isis has long been the refuge for the LGBTQIA+ community. Her temple priests were by most historical accounts gay, as many priests of goddesses were historically.

Loki – Norse
In Norse mythology, Loki (who is known as a shapeshifter) regularly changes into a female, giving birth to the eight-legged horse, Sleipnir.

Mary – Hebrew
There is merit to including a biblical figure here. As a later adaption to the Mesopotamian goddess Innana, Hecate through to Isis, then Aphrodite, Mary can be considered to be one of the latest incarnations of a very ancient goddess. Mother deities have always been a port of safety and security to the LGBTQIA+ community.

Pan – Greece
As a god of fertility, Pan is known in many stories as having sexual relations with males and females. One of the most well-known stories is a relationship with the handsome young shepherd, Daphnis.

Ra / Raet – Egypt
The Egyptian Sun God had a female counterpart. Though much is unknown about Raet, the general consensus is that they are one and the same.

Rainbow Serpent – Australia
The Aboriginals have many names for the great snake that created the world and its inhabitants. As you'd expect from a giant land mass with up to 363 languages, the stories do have considerable variation but, as a true shapeshifter, this snake is generally seen as both male and female.

Seth / Set, Horus and Thoth – Egypt

These three gods have been placed together in order to showcase the relationship between them. In mythology, Horus and Seth are depicted as being bonded in some way. Thoth is subsequently born from Seth's forehead by Horus' semen. You can read within this family bonding the unifying of Upper and Lower Egypt (and bringing with it wisdom).

Tu Shen – China

This Taoist deity of gay men and relationships was also known as the Rabbit God. Throughout the history of China, Tu Shen's followers have met with many forms of adversity, even being banned by some Emperors. More recently, Tu Shen is gaining a new following, thanks to movies like 'Kiss of the Rabbit God.'

Vishnu / Mohini – India

This creator god regularly took the shape of his female avatar, Mohini. Regarded by his followers as gender-fluid in a modern sense.

Xochipilli (Prince of Flowers) – Mexico

In the lands ruled by the Aztecs, this god was a specific guide and protector of male prostitutes.

LGBTQIA+ DEITIES

Zeus – Greece

This Greek 'father of the gods' took more lovers than all of the rest of Olympus together! Mainly known for his love of young women, he was also known for his love of the cup-bearer: the mortal boy, Ganymede. Paiderestia was a common practice in Greece, with its custom coming from this mythological relationship. Men generally took on a young male, not just for a sexual relationship, but as a teacher of what was expected of a Greek man.

I'm sure if you explore the world's deities you will find many more examples of LGBTQIA+ behaviour. Inevitably, some mythologies have to be read through the lens of their monastic scribes. By looking at the mythologies of, for example Norse, Germanic and Celtic deities, we may be able to better understand the deeper cultural roots and the roles the LGBTQIA+ community played within their culture.

Epilogue

Scotland is now a world leader on LGBTQIA+ rights and the Pagan Federation are incredibly proud to have been part of that journey. As we head towards the 50th anniversary of the Pagan Federation, and the 30th anniversary of the Pagan Federation here in Scotland, we must look at what we have achieved so far, alongside all we wish to achieve in the future. Diversity is in all things in life and in Nature, and we should pride ourselves that, as a faith representative organisation, as well as a faith community, the SPF welcomes all people, regardless of gender and sexuality and that we work tirelessly to ensure they are represented and supported in all areas of life.

The Scottish Pagan Federation has a proud history of campaigning alongside a great many other groups for equal rights and recognition for the LGBTQIA+ community. Since our inception as an organisation, we have been at the forefront of that movement as a faith community. A major part of that was making marriage equality one of our biggest campaigns over the last few decades; this involved collaborating and partnering with other groups and communities, helping to change attitudes within wider society and, in doing so, ensuring its victory.

In 2015, we saw the culmination of those efforts as SPF-approved Celebrant, Louise Park, performed the UK's first legal Pagan same-sex wedding ceremony – for the wonderful Iain and Tom Robertson-Lanting, two great ambassadors for the Pagan community, one of whom is responsible for the book you now hold in your hands. Moreover, it was pointed out only recently that this was not only the UK's first legal Pagan same-sex wedding, but the UK's first legal same-sex religious wedding (rather than a civil wedding). At a time when some religious denominations in Scotland still do not permit same-sex weddings to be performed by their clergy, in the area of LGBTQIA+ rights and recognition, Scottish Pagans are clearly leading by example.

When I started my work as an activist in the Scottish Pagan Federation, around the same time as we won the right to conduct the first legal same-sex wedding, one of my first acts as an Officer of the SPF was to commission and design a Scottish PF flag and banner. The intention was

EPILOGUE

that members of the SPF would be able to carry it when marching at Pride events across Scotland, in order to represent our faith community. The flag itself was first proposed by Bren McNeil, our local Pagan organiser for Glasgow, and a wonderful Pagan activist in his own right. Bren was also the founder of the Scottish Pagan LGBTQIA+ Social Networking Group.

The Pride flag's first outing was just a few years after this, at a Scottish Pride event in Edinburgh. It felt incredibly poignant that both Iain and Tom Robertson-Lanting were the first Pagans to lift and carry the new Scottish PF banner, and to make our Pagan presence at Pride even more visible than before.

Pride is Scotland's largest lesbian, gay, bisexual, transgender, queer and intersex celebration and our presence at Pride events helps to raise the visibility and profile of the Scottish PF. It lets people see how incredibly important LGBTQIA+ rights and recognition are to us as Pagans and as an organisation. The SPF stands for respect and tolerance for all, and it was great to be visibly present and representing an entire faith community at the marches. From the reactions on the day, it meant a great deal to lots of other people too. It was wonderful to see so many Pagans join in the marches in both Glasgow and in Edinburgh that year, and in the years that have followed.

The Scottish Pagan Federation has always been a trailblazer for LGBTQIA+ rights and recognition. 2015 also saw us continue on that journey: joining forces with three other faith communities to host the first ever Interfaith Conference on 'Exploring Spirituality, Sexuality and Gender,' which provided a safe space for trans, queer, gay, bi and gender-fluid people of faith to come together and to celebrate our diversity.

For this event, we were able to join forces with the Quakers, the Metropolitan Community Church, and QUEST (the LGBTQIA+ support arm of the Roman Catholic Church). This brought our different faith communities together to show that gender transcends boundaries, breaks down barriers, and can unite us if we acknowledge and celebrate our diversity, instead of letting it cause division.

The lead organiser of that event was our Glasgow Pagan Interfaith Officer, Linda Haggerstone – another inspiration activist for LGBTQIA+ rights and recognition. Last year, Linda became the UK's first ever LGBTQIA+ University Chaplain. Yet another first for Paganism and another example of how, in the area of LGBTQIA+ rights and recognition, Scottish Pagans are leading by example.

As a faith community, Paganism also has the highest percentage of people identifying as gender non-binary in the UK. The figures from 'Non-binary People's Experiences in the UK,' published by Scottish Trans Alliance, based on their 2015 survey results, puts this at 12.8%. The next highest percentage, at 11%, was from Christianity but this included adherents from the Church of England, Church of Scotland, Roman Catholic, Protestant and all other Christian denominations.

As a faith community, Pagans are in a minority. So, with our percentage for this identification being higher than every denomination of Christianity combined, this paints a very strong picture of the number of trans and gender-fluid members of our community. The SPF recognises that we have a duty of care to protect and support this part of our community. This led us to submitting a strongly worded letter of support to the Scottish Government's consultation on the reform of the Gender Recognition Act – not just as individuals, but as an entire faith community.

This diversity is also reflected within the Pagan Federation itself, not just in Scotland but across the UK and in our allied organisations in Europe. Indeed, many of our most prominent

Officers, Celebrants, District Managers, Local and Regional Officers identify as gay, bisexual, trans, and gender-fluid, or fit somewhere along the LGBTQIA+ spectrum. As a faith organisation, we welcome this diversity with open arms, as by recognising and honouring our differences we can become truly inclusive and better serve our community at large.

I myself identify as non-binary and when I took over as Presiding Officer in 2018, as far as I am aware, I became the first non-binary faith leader in Scotland. I had already been leading and organising meetings and discussion groups on 'Gender Identity within Paganism' in my own moot, and have since been able to bring this subject to the entire community at our annual conference, where it ended up being one of our best-attended events at the conference itself.

Being in this position as Presiding Officer means that I get invited to attend and speak at events for LGBTQIA+ people of faith across Scotland. This provides me with the opportunity to demonstrate that leaders of faith organisations can be out *and* proud, we don't need to hide our sexuality or gender identify because of our religion. Indeed, I spoke only last year at the 'How Queer is Religion?' Interfaith LGBTQIA+ Panel, which was sponsored by Leap Sports and part of

EPILOGUE

the events at Pride House during the European Championships.

During the same time period, the Pagan Federation of England and Wales also elected their first Asexual President. Diverse leadership is not something we elect consciously; as I have already noted, in contrast to many other faith representative organisations, Paganism has always had great diversity within our leaders and this is something that, as Pagans, we celebrate.

Today, the SPF also has more LGBTQIA+ Pagan Celebrants than ever before, having just doubled our Celebrant numbers from last year. All SPF-approved celebrants are able to conduct full legal Pagan same-sex (as well as opposite-sex) weddings here in Scotland. I was honoured to become a Legal Celebrant in January 2021 myself, and already have my first same-sex wedding booked for later in the year.

Over the past few years, under my leadership, the Scottish PF has made LGBTQIA+ rights and recognition one of our top priorities. One of my first acts as Presiding Officer was to elect our first LGBTQIA+ Officer, Tom Lanting, who, as I have already noted, is responsible for this book. Tom has been an inspiration since he took on that role; he has made it his own, running Pagan LGBTQIA+ drop-in sessions across both the east and west of Scotland, as well as chairing LGBTQIA+ discussion groups at our annual SPF Conferences.

As a faith community ourselves, Pagans are no strangers to prejudice and discrimination from sections of the general public and the media. This has been the lamentable case for much of modern Paganism's history and most Pagans have first-hand experience of what it feels like to be the target of derision and ridicule for living our lives as we truly are.

Scotland is now a world leader on LGBTQIA+ rights and the SPF are deeply privileged to have been an intrinsic part of that journey. The Scottish Pagan Federation stands for respect and tolerance for all. We stand with our LGBTQIA+ brothers, sisters and non-binary friends, partners and family members. By standing together, we are stronger.

Thank you

Stephen Haggerty

Current Presiding Officer
Scottish Pagan Federation Presiding Officer
2018–Present

APPENDIX
References, Resources & Bibliography

BIBLIOGRAPHY

The Three Principles of the SPF were written by John Macintyre and were adjusted in 2019 with public consultation.

Alpert, S.G. (2013) 'Borneo: The Island – Its People' in Scheford, R. (Ed) in collaboration with Alpert, S. *Eyes of the Ancestors: The Arts of Island Southeast Asia at the Dallas Museum of Art*. Yale University Press, New Haven and London.

Conner, R.P.; Sparks, D.H. & Sparks, M. (1998) *Cassell's Encyclopedia of Queer Myth, Symbol and Spirit*. Cassell, London.

Hallakarva, G. *The Vikings and Homosexuality*.

Indian Health Service. *The Federal Health Program for American Indians and Alaska Natives*.

Leap, W. & Boellstorff, T. (2004) *Speaking in Queer Tongues: Globalization and Gay Language.* University of Illinois Press.

Murray, S.O. & Roscoe, W. (1997) *Islamic Homosexualities: Culture, History and Literature.* NYU Press.

Ross, M.C. (1998) *Prolonged Echoes: Old Norse Myths in Medieval Northern Society.* Northern Studies, Odense University Press.

Westervelt, W. (1999) *Hawaiian Legends of Volcanoes.* Mutual Publishing.

Williams, H. (compiler) (1832) *The Dictionary of the Māori Language.*

The Equality Network Handbook (2019).

REFERENCES & RESOURCES

This is a list of reference sites that are great tools to learn from not just for the LGBTQIA+ community but also the general public. Below are sites where you can learn even more on sexualities, sexual health, your rights in the workplace, as well as education tools for schools.

The following websites were correct as of 11th November, 2020:

REFERENCES, RESOURCES & BIBLIOGRAPHY

Health & Well-being:

Equality Network – https://www.equality-network.org/

LGBT Youth Scotland – https://www.lgbtyouth.org.uk/

LGBT Centre for Health & Well-being – http://www.lgbthealth.org.uk/

Mind Out – https://mindout.org.uk/

Scottish Trans Alliance – https://www.scottishtrans.org/link-categories/scottish-l

Stonewall – https://www.stonewall.org.uk

Switchboard – https://switchboard.lgbt/

Terrance Higgins Trust – https://www.tht.org.uk/

For Parents & School's:

Mermaids UK – https://mermaidsuk.org.uk/

https://www.diversityrolemodels.org/

https://www.facebook.com/shaundellentycelebratingdifference/

http://www.schools-out.org.uk/

Anti-Bullying:

https://www.justlikeus.org/

Legal & Workplace Tools:

https://pridelegal.com/scotland-lgbt-laws/

https://www.tuc.org.uk/sites/default/files/tucfiles/lgbt_equality_at_work_2013_online.pdf

http://www.usdaw.org.uk/CMSPages/GetFile.aspx?guid=3a3438bd-f8ff-4f2c-b7e4-652d50c89d75

https://assets.publishing.service.gov.uk/government/uploads/system/uploads/attachment_data/file/85515/LGBT-equality-workplace.pdf

BOOKS THAT MAY BE OF INTEREST

Death and Bereavement:

- *The Pagan Book of Living and Dying* by Starhawk.
- *The Journey into Spirit* by Kristoffer Hughes.

Addiction:

The Pagan in Recovery by Deirdre A. Hebert.

REFERENCES, RESOURCES & BIBLIOGRAPHY

LGBTQIA+:

- *Gay Witchcraft* by Christopher Penczak.
- *Queer Magick* by Tomas Prower.
- *Queering Your Craft* by Cassandra Snow.

Trauma:

- *The Body Keeps the Score* by Bessel Van Der Kolk.

RESOURCES AND ORGANISATIONS

Samaritans – (116 123)
24/7 – https://www.samaritans.org/
Samaritans offer a free confidential phone line for people to talk when they need to.

Breathing Space Scotland – (0800 83 85 87)
Mon–Thurs 6pm–2am and Friday 6pm–Monday 6am
https://breathingspace.scot/
Breathing Space offers a free confidential phone line for people to talk.

Shout – (85258)
https://giveusashout.org/
A free 24/7 text number for anyone struggling to cope which offers the opportunity to communicate with someone by text messaging.

Age UK – (0800 678 1602)
8am–7pm daily – https://www.ageuk.org.uk/
A charity which offers support, information and more to older people.

LGBTQIA+ Switchboard – (0300 330 0630)
10am–10pm daily – https://switchboard.lgbt
Offering support to LGBTQIA+ people.

PHOTO CREDIT

Wrap around cover – Rainbow on Loch Lomond. Supplied and taken by multi award winning Scottish landscape photographer, Neil Pitchford of Awen Photos.

https://www.facebook.com/awen.photos
www.scotsawen.me

Acknowledgments

Thank you to John, Steffy & Matt, for your contributions.

Thank you to Helen, Kitty & Jules, for your awesome editing skills.

Thank you to Neil Pitchford, for the amazing cover picture.

Thank you everyone from our Rainbow community, for your contributions.

And lastly, a big THANK YOU to my wonderful husband, Iain, for encouraging me to write this book.

Milton Keynes UK
Ingram Content Group UK Ltd.
UKHW021137010324
438715UK00010B/609